T. REX'S BATTLE

By Brad Fossil

Creative Editor: Christian Darkin

Copyright 2024 By Christian Darkin
All rights reserved. This book or any portion thereof may not be reproduced or used in any manner whatsoever without the express written permission of the publisher except for the use of brief quotations in a book

Contents

Contents 3

Chapter 1 5

Chapter 2 17

Chapter 3 25

Chapter 4 31

Chapter 5 35

Chapter 6 41

Chapter 7 49

Chapter 8 55

Chapter 9 59

Chapter 10 63

Chapter 11 71

Chapter 12 79

Chapter 13 85

Chapter 14 91

Tara's World 95

Other Animal Stories.................... 101
Trilobite's Journey: Chapter 1 105

Chapter 1

North America. 68 Million Years Ago…

In the heart of a dense, cretaceous forest, the early morning light crept through the towering ferns and ancient trees. The air was fresh and filled with the sounds of a world waking up. Deep within this lush world, under a canopy of green, lay a huge nest. It was a large, circular structure, two metres in diameter, a ring of mud scraped up into a protective dish and filled with branches. It sat in a shallow depression in the earth, carefully chosen for its concealment and protection.

At the centre of the nest were two enormous eggs, each the size of a large watermelon. Their surfaces were rough, with a texture resembling cracked leather, and speckled with shades of brown and green. The shells were thick – thick enough to protect the precious life growing inside, strong enough to withstand the weight of a watchful parent but today, they would break.

The area around the nest was trampled down, the signs of a massive creature's regular visits evident in the deep, heavy footprints imprinted into the soil. These tracks painted a clear picture of the diligent care the mother took of her nest.

Around the perimeter of the nest, the detritus of the forest lay scattered - broken branches, fallen leaves, and the occasional feather from a passing bird. This debris added another layer of disguise, blending the into, was robust and well-portioned, with sturdy legs that suggested power and speed. Covering Tara's skin was a fine coat of fluffy feathers which were a mottled blend of earthy browns and soft greens. They camouflaged her almost perfectly against the forest floor.

She raised her large, heavy head and looked around with curious eyes that glimmered. Her snout sniffed the air, and she opened her mouth and yawned. Rows of tiny, sharp teeth glittered in the sun.

The forest was a blur of colours to Tara's new eyes. Green leaves waved above, and the sunlight cast dappled patterns on the ground. Slowly things came into focus.

Around her, the forest was alive. Tiny lizards skittered in the underbrush, and high above, pterosaurs nest into the f[...] and decay.

One of t[...] shake. Tiny crac[...] surface, spreading l[...] Inside, something pus[...] hard shell. With a final [...] snout broke through, gas[...] first breath of cool, damp ai[...]

Tara the Tyrannosaurus [...] still for a moment, her newly op[...] eyes adjusting to the dim light filter[...] through the dense foliage.

She wriggled, pushing more of her body out of the egg. Her tiny arms, already strong, clawed at the edges, tearing the shell apart. She tumbled out onto the soft nest, a ball of damp feathers and heaving breaths.

Tara was small, roughly the size of a turkey. Her body, though tiny in comparison to the adult she would grow into, was robust and well-proportioned, with sturdy legs that suggested power and speed. Covering Tara's skin was a fine coat of fluffy feathers which were a mottled blend of earthy browns and soft greens. They camouflaged her almost perfectly against the forest floor.

She raised her large, heavy head and looked around with curious eyes that glimmered. Her snout sniffed the air, and she opened her mouth and yawned. Rows of tiny, sharp teeth glittered in the sun.

The forest was a blur of colours to Tara's new eyes. Green leaves waved above, and the sunlight cast dappled patterns on the ground. Slowly things came into focus.

Around her, the forest was alive. Tiny lizards skittered in the underbrush, and high above, pterosaurs nest into the forest floor's mosaic of life and decay.

One of these eggs began to shake. Tiny cracks appeared on its surface, spreading like a spider's web. Inside, something pushed against the hard shell. With a final effort, a small snout broke through, gasping for its first breath of cool, damp air.

Tara the Tyrannosaurus Rex lay still for a moment, her newly opened eyes adjusting to the dim light filtering through the dense foliage.

She wriggled, pushing more of her body out of the egg. Her tiny arms, already strong, clawed at the edges, tearing the shell apart. She tumbled out onto the soft nest, a ball of damp feathers and heaving breaths.

Tara was small, roughly the size of a turkey. Her body, though tiny in comparison to the adult she would soared between the gaps in the canopy. The distant roar of larger dinosaurs echoed.

Nearby, the other egg rocked and trembled as another young T. rex prepared to emerge.

With unsteady legs, Tara rose. Her movements were clumsy. The world around her was vast, a maze of towering ferns and wide, ancient trunks. She stumbled, her tail swaying to balance her small, hefty body.

A shadow passed over the nest, and from nowhere, there was her mother, a towering figure, looming over her.

Tara's eyes struggled to focus on the huge shape. The massive head turned towards the nest, her eyes observing her baby. She let out a low, rumbling sound which shook the earth.

The air was filled with the scents of the forest: the earthy aroma of damp soil, the fresh scent of leaves, and something else – a hint of something wild and untamed. Tara sniffed the air.

Hunger gnawed at her belly. She had never eaten before, but instinct told her she needed food. The forest around her teemed with life, small creatures that scurried and buzzed. A part of her wanted to struggle out of the nest and chase them, but she didn't know why.

Her mother stepped closer, her massive feet thudding softly on the forest floor. In her mouth, she carried a prize: a chunk of meat. It was soft and red. She carefully laid it down in the nest, and Tara's eyes widened. It smelled hot and thick.

She staggered towards it, sniffed it, and then opened her mouth and sank her teeth into the raw flesh, wrenching it back and forth to tear a piece off, then swallowing it whole. The taste was powerful, salty.

Behind her another hatchling, was freeing itself from its shell. Tarok's egg rocked back and forth. His legs kicked, sending cracks racing across the surface. Finally, with a small grunt, he broke free, his small body tumbling into the nest beside his sister.

Tarok blinked, his eyes wide as the sounds of rustling leaves and distant calls filled his ears. Their mother loomed over them, her massive form protective and warm. She lowered her head, her nose gently touching each hatchling in turn. They responded, pressing their tiny noses back against her, the comforting scent of their mother filling their senses.

Tarak spotted the food, and dived at it, grabbing a chunk of his own. The two siblings were a flurry of movement and noise, jostling each other for the best scraps. Tara pushed her way through, her tiny jaws snapping instinctively at her brother

The meal was a frenzy, each hatchling tearing at the flesh, driven by hunger and instinct. Tara bit and clawed, tasting the meat, and feeling the strength it gave her. She gulped down mouthful after mouthful until there was nothing left in the nest but feathers and bits of shell still clinging to their wet bodies.

After their meal, their mother pushed the baby dinosaurs to the edge of the nest, nudging them with her nose.

Tara was first out into the world. The forest floor was a patchwork of light and shadow, filled with strange and wondrous things.

The two wandered in the small clearing. Tara found a pool of water, its surface calm and reflective. She peered into it, seeing her own reflection for the first time. She cocked her head, watching as the tiny reflection did the same. Then, with a splash, she stepped into the pool, sending ripples across its surface. The cool water felt good against her skin, washing away the remnants of the egg and her first meal.

Tara's legs were still shaky. Her head felt heavy, but she managed to push it up, her eyes level with the towering ferns that surrounded the nest. Tarok was unsteady too, his tail swinging to balance as he took his first wobbly steps outside the nest. Their mother watched, a silent guardian as they explored the edges of their clearing.

For the first few days of their lives, Tara and Tarok played in the clearing. Tara leapt onto a pile of leaves, pretending it was a small creature she had caught. Tarok crept through the underbrush, his eyes fixed on his sister, learning how to move quietly, how to surprise.

Tara chased a lizard. It was fast, but she was faster. She learned to predict where it would dart next. Tarok snapped at flying insects, each catch sharpening his reactions. With each attempt, they grew more skilled, more confident.

As night fell, the hatchlings would return to the nest, under the protective gaze of their mother. They would curl up beside her, her warmth a promise of safety. In the shelter of the ancient forest,

Tara and Tarok fell into a deep sleep.

Tara and Tarok fell into a deep sleep.

Chapter 2

Tara blinked sleepily as her mother nudged her awake. The night was dark, the moon a thin crescent barely lighting up the sky. Beside her, Tarok grumbled, unhappy at being woken. Their mother pushed them gently but firmly, urging them out of their nest for the first time at night. Tara's sleepiness quickly turned to a buzz of excitement. The world outside their nest was a mystery, full of shadows and strange sounds in the night.

They stumbled after their mother, trying to keep up with her long strides. The forest was different at night; the familiar sights of the day were now hidden in darkness. Tara's eyes widened as she tried to take in everything. Tarok bumped into her, and she snapped at him, a quiet hiss that their mother quickly silenced with a glare.

Their mother led them through the underbrush, moving silently. Tara and Tarok tried to mimic her, stepping carefully to avoid making noise. Every rustle of leaves made Tara's heart jump. She looked around, half expecting some unseen creature to leap out of the darkness.

They reached the edge of a clearing. Their mother crouched down, and Tara and Tarok followed suit, lying flat on their bellies. Ahead of them, in the clearing, was something they had never seen before.

She looked up at her mother, who was focused intently on the creature in the clearing, her body tense and ready.

In the moonlit glade, grazed a lone hadrosaur, its massive bulk turned away from them.

The hadrosaur stood tall on its hind legs, reaching for the tender leaves of a tree. The long, curved crest on the top of its head was silhouetted against the night sky. Tara and Tarok hid in the bushes, their eyes fixed on the giant creature, their breaths quiet and quick.

Tara watched her mother as she mother crouched low, her muscles tensed like coiled springs. She waited, her eyes locked on the hadrosaur. Then, with a burst of speed that seemed impossible for her size, she charged. The hadrosaur turned, alerted by the thunderous footsteps, and began to run.

The chase was on. The mother T. rex gained on the hadrosaur, her powerful legs propelling her forward. The hadrosaur, panicked and tried to dodge between the trees, but it was too big, too slow. Tara and Tarok watched in awe as their mother closed the gap.

Just as she was about to strike, the hadrosaur made a sudden turn, coming back towards Tara and Tarok hidden in the bushes. The mother T. rex skidded around, barely missing her target. The hadrosaur bolted. Tara could see the panic in its eyes as it barreled straight at her. But the mother T. rex was relentless. She pursued her prey, weaving through the trees with surprising agility.

Finally, with a mighty leap, she clamped her jaws on the back of the hadrosaur's neck. The creature bellowed in terror and pain, thrashing wildly, trying to shake off the predator. But the mother T. rex held on, her teeth sinking deeper. With a powerful tug, she brought the hadrosaur to the ground. The forest echoed with the sounds of the struggle, until, at last, the hadrosaur lay still.

Tara and Tarok crept out of their hiding place, approaching the kill cautiously. Their mother tore a chunk from the dead animal's side, and the stink of fresh blood filled the air. Tara and Tarok hesitated for a moment, then began to feed. Their initial caution gave way to hunger, and soon they were tearing into the flesh, their faces smeared with blood.

As they ate, they played, nipping and growling at each other, mimicking their mother's hunt. For a while, they forgot the world outside their small circle of light under the moon.

Suddenly, Tara heard a low growl behind her. She turned sharply. Emerging from the shadows were four

Troodon, lured by the scent of fresh kill.

Each Troodon had a slender, agile body, covered in a coat of fine feathers that shimmered under the moonlight. Their eyes, large and round, scanned the scene with keen interest. The lead one was just larger than Tara. It stepped in towards her, fanning out its arms in challenge, and tapping its long, curved claw on the forest floor.

The Troodon hissed, opening and snapping its jaw to reveal needle-like teeth

They circled the carcass, edging closer. Their movements became more deliberate, each step measured and silent. Tara watched them, her predatory instincts alert.

Tara and Tarok backed away from the kill, growling, but the

Troodon were not deterred. They were scavengers, used to stealing from larger predators. They inched closer, their eyes fixed on the prize.

Tara stared at the newcomers and did her best to roar. The lead Troodon launched itself towards her, claws reaching out.

That was when Tara's mother chose to act. With a roar that shook the ground, she lunged at the Troodon. Her massive jaws snapped shut inches from the scavenger, sending it scrambling back into the underbrush. The rest of the pack followed, disappearing into the night.

The forest was quiet again. Tara and Tarok, their hearts pounding, returned to their feast. Their mother stood guard, watching over them as they ate.

Chapter 3

Weeks passed. Tara and Tarok grew quickly. They played and fought like any brother and sister, and they even played at hunting, hiding in wait for little creatures before rushing out to tackle them as they'd watched their mother do.

She was always there, hovering in the background, keeping them safe while they played.

One night, after a particularly late hunt, as Tara and Tarok lay beside their mother,

The mother Trex was deep in sleep, snoring loudly, but Tara couldn't sleep. She felt a mix of exhaustion and exhilaration. The forest around them was alive with the sounds of nocturnal creatures, and she couldn't wait to get out there and hunt on her own.

It had been a hot, dry day, and the leaves on the forest floor were brown and brittle.

Suddenly, Tara caught a new scent in her nostrils. It was dark, suffocating. Smoke!

She raised her head. It was stronger now, billowing in clouds into the clearing. She nudged Tarok. He grunted, then sat up.

Through the trees, Tara became aware of an orange glow, far off and blurry.

Her mother stirred too now. With a rumble deep in her throat, she lifted her head and then got to her feet.

The sky darkened, even further. The moon and stars went out, covered suddenly by a thick blanket of billowing smoke that began to blot out the sky. Animals raced past in a flurry of scales, feathers, and fur. Panic was in the air.

Then, with a roar louder than any dinosaur, the fire was upon them. Flames leapt from tree to tree, around the clearing. Tara and Tarok ran. Their powerful legs carried them through the forest, but the fire was faster, angrier. Their mother pushed them forward, her massive form a barrier between her young and the scorching heat.

A blazing branch crashed to the ground, separating Tara and Tarok from their mother. She called out to them, her voice a hoarse wail against the crackling inferno, but the smoke covered her. Tarok, just ahead, paused and looked back.

Tara tried to step back towards the sound, but the heat was too much. She turned and fled, Tarok next to her, out of the forest and across the plains beyond.

They were alone, their mother gone. The fire didn't care. It raged on, devouring everything in its path.

When they had put a safe distance between themselves and the burning forest, they stopped. Tara looked back. The darkness was pierced by the glow of burning trees. The once lush forest was now a blackened wasteland.

Tara and Tarok stumbled on, their energy fading until they found a river. Other forest creatures were gathered there too, survivors of the blaze.

The siblings drank deeply, the cool water soothing their scorched throats.

Eventually, they found a grove of trees nearby, its shadows offering a hiding place. They lay down, their bodies pressed together for comfort and waited for dawn.

Chapter 4

In the morning, the fire had burnt itself out. Tara and Tarok made their way back to the forest to find their mother. Tara's heart pounded as she stepped through the remains of the forest, a stark landscape of ash and silence. Her nose searched for the scent of life, but all she found was the sting of smoke. Beside her, Tarok moved with equal caution, his eyes scanning for any sign of their mother.

In the mid-morning, they came to a clearing. The ground was blackened, and there, amidst the devastation, lay the still, charred form of their mother.

Tara circled the body, her snout close to the ground. Tarok stood motionless, his gaze locked on the figure that had once been their protector. There were no more lessons, no more safety. They were truly alone now.

Hunger gnawed at Tara's belly, pulling her from her grief. She and Tarok exchanged a look. They stuck close together, and ventured deeper into the forest, seeking food among the ruins.

In the charred remains of the forest, Tara and Tarok moved cautiously, their senses heightened in the eerie quiet. The familiar scents and sounds of the forest were gone. There was just a haunting stillness. They searched, driven by hunger and the instinct to survive.

As the sun climbed higher, they stumbled on a small creature rustling in the underbrush. It was a multituberculate, a rodent-like mammal with a thick coat and rounded body. Its tiny eyes darted about nervously, aware of the predators nearby.

Tara and Tarok crouched low, trying to blend into whatever scarce cover the devastated forest provided. They moved slowly, inch by inch, towards the unsuspecting creature. But the leaves were gone. There was nowhere to hide. Tarok stepped on a twig, and in an instant, the multituberculate scurried away, disappearing into a small burrow.

Tara turned and hissed at her brother in frustration.

The siblings continued their search. Before long, they encountered a lone Thescelosaurus, a small, plant eater. Its lean body and swift legs showed it was built for speed. Tara and Tarok coordinated their approach. Tara crept around the flank of the dinosaur while Tarok charged from the front.

But the Thescelosaurus was agile and strong. It dodged Tarok's attack and landed a powerful kick, sending him reeling backwards.

Tara lunged, but the dinosaur was too quick, bolting through the burned trees, and off into the distance. The siblings, outmatched and inexperienced, had no choice but to give up the chase.

Exhausted and hungry, Tara and Tarok pressed on. As evening approached, they came across a grim scene. In an area where fallen trees created a natural trap, scattered among the ashes lay the remains of smaller victims of the forest fire. There were some charred lizards, small mammals, and even a few birds. The corpses were burnt and there wasn't much meat on any of them, but the siblings fed on the smokey remains anyway. The taste of ash was bitter on Tara's tongue.

Chapter 5

Months had passed since the forest fire. Green was returning to the charred landscape. The colossal trees that survived the blaze had already sprouted new, vibrant leaves.

In the gaps left by those who hadn't made it, a bustling undergrowth emerged. Ferns unfurled their fronds towards the sky, and small, fast-growing plants like horsetails and cycads filled the spaces with a lush green carpet. The air was fresh, imbued with the scent of new life. Amongst the emerging gymnosperms and flowering plants, the forest was reclaiming its lost glory, transforming into a dense, lively habitat once more.

Tara and Tarok, much bigger now, were adapting to this revived world. Their bodies had grown; they were no longer the vulnerable hatchlings they once were. Their legs were longer, their jaws stronger, and their senses more acute. They moved together with a purposeful grace, their eyes keenly fixed, through a gap in the ferns, on their next meal.

Their target was a small group of Leptoceratops. Smaller than their famous cousins, the Triceratops, these dinosaurs had a short frill protecting the backs of their necks from the bite of T. rex, and a mouth with a sharp beak, but they lacked the dangerous horns of other ceratopsians. They were a challenge for Tara and Tarok, but one they might just be able to rise to.

Leptoceratops were agile and fast. That made them tricky prey. Tara knew from experience that they could sprint when threatened, and their beaks could deliver powerful bites.

Tara and Tarok observed the Leptoceratops group from the undergrowth. The herbivores grazed peacefully, unaware. Among the group was a younger Leptoceratops, slightly limping, likely due to an old injury. Tara nudged Tarok, and the two focused on the calf.

Tarok crouched low while Tara backed slowly away. Once at a safe distance, she circled around in a wide arc to the front of the grazing Leptoceratops. There she waited.

As the sun emerged from behind a cloud, momentarily blinding the creatures, Tara made her move. In a sudden burst of speed, she charged towards them. The Leptoceratops scattered in a panic, their agility on full display as they darted away. But Tara kept her eye on the calf. It was a little slower to react than the rest. A little clumsier in its running. She switched direction, appearing to chase one of the older, dinosaurs, but in doing so, she blocked the path of the calf which turned and bolted in the other direction, away from the safety of its group.

Tara switched direction again, and the young Leptoceratops found its way out of the trees blocked. It fled the only direction it could – right towards the thicket where Tarok was waiting in ambush.

With a powerful leap from his hiding spot, Tarok closed the distance in seconds. His jaws clamped down on the Leptoceratops, and the young predator hauled its prey into the air, shook it violently and dropped it onto the ground. The Leptoceratops lay still. It was a clean, swift kill.

Tara moved towards the kill to claim her part of the prize. Tarok watched her approach, then stepped in to block her, standing between her and the carcass.

The air was suddenly tense, charged with a new, raw energy. The siblings circled the Leptoceratops carcass, each eyeing the richest cuts of meat.

Tara moved first. With a swift step, she claimed a hefty, meat-laden part of the thigh. Her teeth sank into the flesh, ripping a sizeable chunk away. Tarok watched, his eyes narrowing into slits. A deep, rumbling growl escaped his throat, echoing through the clearing.

The growl was a clear challenge. Tara paused, her eyes locking with Tarok's. She'd done all the work, after all. There was a silent standoff, a battle of wills. For a moment, it seemed as if they might lunge at each other, turning their hunter's instincts on each other.

But the pangs of hunger were stronger than the stirrings of conflict. Reluctantly, Tarok stepped forward, choosing a different part of the carcass. His jaws clamped down on the flesh, tearing away with a force that shook the remains of their prey.

They ate side by side, the tension simmering just below the surface. Their movements were deliberate, territorial. The bond they shared as siblings was still there, but now there was something else too. A silent acknowledgement of emerging rivalry.

Chapter 6

Months passed. Tara and Tarok, nearly fully grown, moved like shadows through the dense undergrowth. Their steps were silent for creatures of their size. The siblings had grown into formidable predators, each over thirty-five feet in length, with muscular legs and jaws capable of crushing bone.

It was a hot, humid afternoon, while tracking a herd of hadrosaurs, Tara's keen eyes caught a different movement. A hulking form, low to the ground but massive in girth, ambled towards the riverbank.

It was an Ankylosaurus, its body covered in bony plates and spikes, with a massive club at the end of its tail. The creature, a walking fortress, was a rare sight, and one that posed a significant challenge. Tara and Tarok had never faced an opponent like this.

Tara signalled to Tarok with a low growl. Their hunting strategy had always been one of stealth and surprise, using their environment to their advantage. The Ankylosaurus, focused on reaching the water to drink, was unaware of the predators. The river, a wide and meandering body of water, flowed gently, its banks muddy and lined with dense foliage.

The siblings split up, moving through the trees to flank their target. Tara approached from one side, her eyes fixed on the Ankylosaurus, while Tarok circled around to the other. The plan was to surprise it, drive it towards the riverbank, and corner it where its mobility would be limited.

Tara emerged from the underbrush, her massive feet thudding

against the ground, drawing the Ankylosaurus's attention. It turned, swinging its tail club defensively. Tara dodged just in time, feeling the whoosh of air as the club missed her head by inches. She roared, a sound that echoed through the forest, as Tarok attacked from the other side, his powerful jaws snapping at the Ankylosaurus's hind leg.

The Ankylosaurus reeled, turning to face Tarok, its tail swinging wildly. Tara used this moment to lunge forward, biting at its neck. But the creature's armour was thick, and her teeth couldn't find a grip. The Ankylosaurus's tail swung again, this time connecting with Tara's side. She felt a sharp pain and stumbled, but quickly regained her footing.

The battle was intense. The Ankylosaurus manoeuvred with surprising speed for its size, keeping its heavily armoured back and deadly tail towards its attackers. Tara and Tarok were relentless, but each attack was met with a counter from the Ankylosaurus.

They gradually manoeuvred the battle towards the riverbank, using their size to herd the Ankylosaurus. The ground grew softer, the mud clinging to their feet. The Ankylosaurus, heavy and less agile, struggled more with the terrain. Tara noticed this and roared to Tarok, signalling him to press harder.

As they reached the bank, the Ankylosaurus found its movements hindered by the mud. Tara saw her opportunity. She charged, forcing the Ankylosaurus closer to the water's edge. Tarok attacked from the side, his jaws aiming for the creature's legs, trying to topple it.

The Ankylosaurus, now desperate, thrashed wildly, its tail club swinging with lethal force. Tara dodged and weaved, her instincts honed from months of hunting, keeping her focus on the creature's less protected underbelly.

From a distance, a group of scavenging Dromaeosaurs watched. These smaller two-legged carnivores couldn't hope to bring down an ankylosaurus themselves, but they would not hesitate to steal a part of the kill if they could. Their sharp eyes tracked every movement, waiting for their chance.

Amidst the chaos, Tarok, eager to end the battle, made a bold move. He lunged forward, aiming for the Ankylosaurus's side. But his attack was hasty, leaving Tara exposed. The Ankylosaurus seized the moment, swinging its massive tail club directly at Tara, who was caught off guard.

The club struck Tara with a thunderous impact, sending a jolt of agony through her body. She felt a sharp pain in her side, her legs buckling under the force. She crashed to the ground, the breath knocked out of her. The world spun, a mix of pain and confusion clouding her senses.

Tarok, seeing Tara injured and vulnerable, hesitated. In that moment, he made the decision to act for himself. Survival instincts took over. Tarok simply turned and fled into the forest, leaving Tara alone and defenceless.

The Dromaeosaurs, sensing an opportunity, closed in on the injured Tyrannosaur. Their sharp strikes jabbed at her, while she struggled to get back on her feet.

This was serious. She snapped at the Dromaeosaurs, her powerful jaws still a formidable weapon. Despite her injury, Tara fought fiercely, and eventually, she managed to get her injured leg underneath her body and push herself upright.

One by one, she managed to drive the Dromaeosaurs away, but the effort left her exhausted and in pain.

Tara limped away from the riverbank, her steps unsteady. Every movement sent waves of pain through her side, but she pushed forward.

As she made her way deeper into the forest, the realization set in- Tarok, her brother and companion since birth, had abandoned her. The world felt different, more dangerous, and unforgiving.

Tara found a secluded spot under a large tree, her breathing heavy and laboured. She lay there, injured and hungry. The split with Tarok was final; their paths had diverged forever. In the quiet of the forest, under the canopy of ancient trees, Tara faced the reality. For the first time in her life, she was truly alone.

Chapter 7

Tara limped through the dense underbrush of the forest, her right leg aching with every step. She scanned the area for any sign of easy prey. Her stomach growled.

Ahead, a small, agile Ornithomimus pecked at the ground, oblivious to the lurking danger. It was scrawny, thin, not much more than a few bites, but it would have to do. Tara crouched, her eyes fixed on the creature. She needed to be swift and precise. With a deep breath, she launched herself towards the unsuspecting prey.

But her injured leg betrayed her. The Ornithomimus, startled by her approach, darted away with astonishing speed. Tara stumbled, her jaws snapping shut on empty air. She let out a low growl of frustration.

Lying there, Tara took a moment to catch her breath. Her injured leg could now barely support her weight. She pushed herself up, sending jolts of pain through her body.

Tara trudged on. She, headed, out of the forest and down to the riverbank again. She couldn't give up. Not yet.

This time she picked a spot a couple of kilometers up-river from where she had ambushed the Ankylosaurus. Here, the river turned a corner and broadened out. It was wide, shallow and slow-moving.

She knew that here, carcasses sometimes washed ashore, maybe there would be an opportunity for an easier meal. The smell of rot and decay filled the air, leading her to the remains of an Edmontosaurus. It lay there, half-submerged in the water, its flesh already torn and eaten away.

Pterosaurs circled overhead, their piercing cries echoing through the sky. They were always the first at an abandoned kill, and they had claimed this one for themselves. Tara approached cautiously, her eyes on the scavenging reptiles' dagger-like beaks.

As Tara neared the carcass, the Pterosaurs dove down, their beaks snapping aggressively. She swiped at them with her massive head, her teeth tearing through the air. The pterosaurs retreated momentarily but returned quickly, determined to defend their find.

Tara stepped into the river. It reached her ankles. She looked down at the Edmontosaurus. It looked like it had been in the water for a long time.

The flesh that was left was white and bloated.

She took a bite. It didn't taste good, but she swallowed it.

Above her, the Pterosaurs were getting braver. The biggest of them swooped down. She felt the leathery wings slap her face. The Pterosaur pecked at the carcass before flying off.

The rest of its companions saw their chance and suddenly there were dozens of them swarming around the dead animal. Despite her size and strength, Tara found herself in a standoff with the persistent Pterosaurs. She managed to take a few bites from the carcass, the rotten flesh tasting bitter in her mouth. It was nothing like the fresh kills she was used to, but it was food at least.

The Pterosaurs continued to harass her, diving and pecking. Tara eventually decided the meal wasn't worth the constant battle. She took one last bite, swallowing a front leg whole, and backed away, leaving the Pterosaurs to their spoils.

Her belly partially filled, Tara waded out across the river that marked the edge of her and Tarok's territory.

She would have to venture further now if she was to survive without her hunting partner. The thought of leaving her familiar hunting grounds filled her with unease, but she limped onto the far side of the river and stepped out onto the open, flat plain beyond.

Tara paused at the edge of her territory, looking back at the forest where she was born. A deep, primal part of her urged her to turn back, to return to the safety of the known. But the harsh reality of her situation pushed

53

her forward, into the uncharted and intimidating expanse of the plains.

She shook the water from her scales and walked on. She was in uncharted territory now. She could hear the calls of creatures she didn't recognize. She was no longer the hunter. She was just another creature trying to survive.

Chapter 8

In the distance, a herd of Triceratops were baying and calling. Tara sniffed the air. They were massive creatures, their bulky bodies dotted with patches of tough, leathery skin. Their large frills and three prominent horns made them unmistakable even from afar.

There was something odd about their behaviour. Tara limped closer. A young Triceratops lay on the ground, its still form surrounded by the rest of the herd, who were on high alert.

As Tara approached, her nostrils flared, picking up the scent of the freshly dead youngster. There were no signs of other predators. Perhaps it had just died in a fight with one of its own kind. Triceratops were heavily armed and aggressive especially now, during the mating season.

The Triceratops herd was formidable, and in her current state, she knew a direct confrontation would be dangerous. Perhaps she could get close enough to grab the calf.

One of the larger Triceratops, likely the leader of the herd, noticed her. It bellowed a warning, a deep, resonating sound. Tara hesitated, her predatory instincts clashing with the pain that throbbed in her leg.

But hunger pushed her onward. She edged closer to the carcass, moving slowly, deliberately. Her eyes were fixed on the fallen Triceratops.

As she neared, the leader of the herd charged. Tara barely dodged, her agility hampered by her injury.

The Triceratops pursued her briefly, and a couple of others joined the chase. She backed off. There was no sense risking those horns. Another injury would mean the end of her.

The Triceratops soon gave up the chase, returning to their fallen member.

Tara found a secluded spot near a small grove of trees. She lay down, her body exhausted from the day's events. The vast plains stretched around her, a new and challenging world.

As night fell, the plains grew quiet, save for the distant mournful calls of the Triceratops herd. Tara closed her eyes.

Her life had changed. She knew she would have to be cautious and clever to survive.

Chapter 9

Turok moved with a quiet confidence. The air was cool and damp, filled with the sounds of distant calls of other dinosaurs and the rustling leaves.

Turok's eyes scanned the underbrush. His senses were sharp. With his sister out of the way, he would no longer have to share his kills. He could smell the earthy scent of plants and the faint trace of other creatures. He listened, his head tilting slightly as he caught the sound of movement nearby.

Ahead, a herd of Pachycephalosaurs grazed in a small clearing. They were smaller than Turok, their bodies covered in scaly skin. Their thick, domed skulls were like armoured clubs. They shone in the sunlight. Turok watched them, his eyes narrowing as he picked out a younger one that had strayed a little way from the group.

Silently, he crept closer, using the trees and bushes to hide his approach. His massive feet made little sound on the soft forest floor. The young Pachycephalosaurus was unaware of the danger, its attention focused on nibbling at some low-hanging leaves.

In a sudden burst of speed, Turok charged. The forest erupted in noise as the startled Pachycephalosaurs scattered. The young one tried to run, but Turok was too fast. He caught up with it in a few strides, his powerful jaws snapping shut. The Pachycephalosaurus cried out, swinging its head in an attempt to fend off its attacker. It struck Turok on the side, but he barely flinched at the impact.

With a powerful tug, Turok brought the struggling creature to the ground. It kicked and thrashed, trying to free itself, but Turok's grip was unyielding. He bit down harder. The Pachycephalosaurus's movements grew weaker as Turok held on, his eyes cold and unrelenting.

Finally, the struggle ended. Turok released his grip, the lifeless body of the Pachycephalosaurus lying at his feet. He looked around, the rest of the herd had fled. He was alone with his kill. Turok bent his head and began to feed.

Smaller dinosaurs, like the feathered Microraptors and the quick-moving Compsognathus, peered out from their hiding places, watching Turok warily, waiting to grab whatever the Tyrannosaurus left for them.

Turok found a quiet spot near a small stream. The water was cool and clear, flowing gently over smooth stones. He drank deeply, then lay down beside the stream, his body relaxing as he settled into the soft earth. He was alone, and that was how he liked it.

Chapter 10

Tara lay motionless on the vast, open plains, her breath slow and deliberate, eyes scanning the horizon. The injury to her leg, had begun to heal over the past month, but she was far from fully recovered. Each step sent a jolt of pain through her, a sharp reminder of her vulnerability. The once powerful limb now forced her to move with caution. She couldn't chase anything. And that meant that on the open plains, where prey could see her coming, she couldn't hunt.

For weeks, Tara had teetered on the brink of starvation. She had survived on the scantiest of meals - a few unlucky mammals, some lazy pterosaurs, and the leftovers from other predators' kills, far from satisfying her immense hunger. She was thin, the ridges on her spine becoming more pronounced under her scaly skin.

This constant hunger gnawed at her, driving her actions with an urgency she had never known before. She needed a substantial meal, and she needed it now. This was not just about satisfying hunger; it was about survival.

A sudden flurry of movement caught Tara's eye. It was the pack of Dromaeosaurs, the same ones she had seen at the river. She recognised their leader, commanding the group with unmistakable dominance.

Tara watched as the pack moved with sleek, coordinated precision, encircling a lone Triceratops.

Tara watched intently, her hunter's instinct awakened. She stood slowly, and moved a little closer, keeping her body low to the ground and a clump of trees between her and the hunt.

The Triceratops, though strong and robust, was clearly overwhelmed. It swung its massive head, trying to ward off its attackers, but the Dromaeosaurs were too agile, too relentless. They darted around it, nipping and tearing, their sharp teeth and claws working in unison to exhaust the mighty herbivore.

Tara crept closer, using the cover of scattered bushes to mask her approach. She moved slowly, deliberately, her large frame surprisingly quiet against the soft earth. Her eyes never left the unfolding drama.

The lead Dromaeosaur, sensing the Triceratops' weakening resolve, judged the moment for the final assault.

In a burst of speed and ferocity, it leapt onto the Triceratops' back, its jaws clamping down between the neck and the frill which protected it. The Triceratops bellowed in pain and stumbled, its legs giving way. With the leader firmly attached to its back, the rest of the pack piled in, swarming the fallen giant.

As the Dromaeosaurs were preoccupied with their kill, tearing into the Triceratops with frenzied excitement, Tara seized her opportunity. She had crept within striking distance, her presence still unnoticed. The tall bushes and her cautious approach had kept her hidden. Now, mere meters away from the distracted pack, Tara readied herself.

The lead Dromaeosaur, its attention fully on the kill, was the first to sense her. It lifted its bloodied snout, scanning the surroundings. But it was too late. Tara had already made her move.

She knew she couldn't take on the whole pack in her condition. Her only chance was a bluff. She had to use fear and raw power to scare them off. Send a signal that would make them think twice before tackling her.

Tara stood, rising to her full height. She took a breath and bellowed, a roar which shook the ground. The Dromaeosaurs hissed and circled, but they were cautious. Tara stood tall, her injured leg tense but supporting her weight. She roared again, a sound that echoed across the plains, asserting her presence.

It wasn't working. The lead Dromaeosaur, stepped forward, opening his jaws and flexing the claws on his arms. Tara turned and faced it head-on.

With a sudden burst of energy, she lunged at the creature. The

Dromaeosaur was quick, but Tara was quicker. She caught it in her jaws, lifted it clean off the ground, and swivelled, hurling the creature four metres through the air. Its body crashed to the ground.

Their leader gone, the rest of the pack scattered in all directions, abandoning the kill.

Tara ignored the lifeless Dromaeosaur leader and turned her attention to the Triceratops. She began to eat, her hunger driving her. She tore through the tough skin, gulping down huge chunks of the rich, much-needed meat.

After eating her fill, Tara rested beside the carcass. Her body felt stronger, her energy returning. She gazed across the plains, her domain. She saw herds of Edmontosaurus in the distance, grazing peacefully. A Pterosaur glided overhead, its shadow fleeting across the ground.

This was her world now, and she was finding her place in it. She had proven herself capable, even with her injury. She was adapting, surviving.

Chapter 11

Months later, and Tara, had grown accustomed to the rhythms of the plains. The sharp pain in her leg had receded. It, was just a dull ache now, a niggling reminder. Today, she was strong, well-fed, and relaxed.

As she approached the river, her massive feet thudded softly on the lush, green ferns. The river today was calm and slow and it had become a hub of activity. Various creatures, from towering long-necked Alamosaurus to the swift, skittish Gallimimus, were lined up along its banks, drinking.

Tara walked down to the water's edge. The other dinosaurs kept their distance, but they could sense she was not hunting today. They carried on drinking.

She paused at the water's edge, her massive head lowering to drink. Her reflection rippled in the water. She was older now, wiser, stronger.

After quenching her thirst, Tara moved downriver to a wider section of the riverbank. Here, she found what she was looking for – a large, gooey mud wallow.

With a low, rumbling grunt, Tara stepped into the mud. It squelched and oozed between her toes, cool and soothing. Slowly, she lowered her body into the mud, the soft material enveloping her. She wriggled slightly, adjusting her position, allowing the mud to coat her rough, scaly skin. This wasn't just about enjoyment; the mud helped care for her skin and soothe the lingering soreness in her leg.

Fully immersed, Tara closed her eyes, savouring the sensation, then rolled over, coating herself in mud.

Around her, life continued. A few from the plain's massive herd of Triceratops cautiously approached the river further downstream. Their wary eyes glanced in her direction. A flock of small, agile birds flitted around, chirping and twittering. The world was alive with sound and movement. Tara slapped her tail against the mud, sending a splash of it up over her back.

After some time, feeling refreshed, Tara heaved herself out of the mud. It dripped and slid off her in thick globs as she lumbered onto dry land. She shook her body vigorously, sending clumps of mud flying in all directions.

Tara settled under a large, leafy tree near the riverbank. The shade was pleasant, the air filled with the tranquil sounds of the flowing river and distant calls. Her presence was accepted by the other creatures.

As she rested, a group of small, bird-like dinosaurs approached cautiously. They were bold, curious creatures, used to picking around larger dinosaurs. They hopped closer, eyeing Tara with a mix of caution and curiosity. One, braver than the rest, jumped up and perched on Tara's massive head. It began to pick at her teeth, removing bits of leftover food stuck in her massive jaws. Others joined, hopping along her back, pecking gently at her skin, cleaning her of parasites and debris.

Tara remained still, allowing the small creatures to do their work. This cleaning ritual was common; the small dinosaurs got a meal, and she received a much-needed cleaning. She felt the gentle tugs and pulls as they worked, a ticklish sensation that she had grown to tolerate, even find soothing.

On the other side of the river, deep in the dense, shadowed forest where the light struggled to pierce through the thick canopy, Tarok stomped through the trees.

His eyes gleamed with a fierce, light as he surveyed his territory. He had grown considerably, his body was a mountain of muscle and sinew, his jaws capable of delivering a bone-crushing bite. He revelled in his strength, using it not just for hunting but for instilling fear.

His heavy footsteps sent vibrations through the ground. The smaller creatures, from the tiny, scurrying mammals to the agile, feathered dinosaurs, fled at the mere hint of his presence. Even the stout Ankylosaurs kept its distance from him now. It knew the young predator was unpredictable, aggressive.

Tarok's path led him to a clearing where a herd of Gallimimus were feeding. The moment they caught sight of him, they. The herd scattered in all directions, their slender legs carrying them swiftly across the forest floor.

Moving on, Tarok encountered a lone Edmontosaurus. The herbivore, a giant in its own right, froze, its eyes wide with terror. Tarok, sensing its fear, advanced slowly. Suddenly, with a burst of speed that belied his size, he lunged at the Edmontosaurus, his massive jaws crushing its neck. The struggle was brief; Tarok's strength was overwhelming. As the Edmontosaurus fell to the ground, lifeless, Tarok let out a triumphant roar.

As he feasted, the smaller predators and scavengers kept their distance, watching hungrily but too afraid to approach. Tarok, in between bites, would snap at them.

After taking just a few bites of the juiciest chunks of his kill, Tarok abandoned it. This was not about hunger. It was about the kill.

He stalked off into the forest, leaving the rest of the Edmontosaurus to the scavengers.

The jungle around him was unnaturally silent. The creatures that lived here were on constant alert, their behaviours altered by the presence of this fearsome predator.

Chapter 12

Tara moved through the trees that lined the riverbank, her keen eyes locked on her prey. Today, she was tracking an old, battle-scarred Chasmosaurus. The Chasmosaurus was large, with a frilled neck shield patterned in dull reds and yellows and with three prominent horns. She had to be careful. Despite its age, this was still a formidable creature.

The Chasmosaurus was wary and experienced enough to sense a predator's presence. It kept moving, its eyes scanning the woodland. Tara followed persistently. She'd been tracking the old dinosaur for most of the day now.

The Chasmosaurus hadn't seen her, but it sniffed the air, suspiciously, then turned abruptly, and headed down to the riverbank where the water was slow and shallow.

Tara watched as waded into the water, its bulky body sinking up to its shoulders. It lifted its head, keeping its nostrils just above the surface, and pushed on across.

The old beast was clever. The water would mask its smell, and Tara couldn't attack while it was in the river. Wading out would slow her down and remove any advantage surprise and speed gave her.

She waited until it had clambered out at the other side, and vanished into the forest, and then followed, slinking into the water with barely a ripple.

She crossed the river at a slightly deeper spot, not walking, but swimming, her tail pushing her forward, with just her nose above the water.

At the other side, she crawled out, keeping low, and picking up the scent on the other side.

The forest felt odd. It was quieter on this side of the river, the usual sounds of life somehow muted. An uneasy feeling crept over her, a sense of being watched. The smell was familiar too, a scent that stirred half-formed memories. This used to be her territory, the place of her birth, before the fight with the ankylosaurus, before had brother had abandoned her.

She focused on the hunt. The Chasmosaurus was up ahead. She could hear it. It was moving more slowly, its old age and the effort of crossing the water taking its toll. Tara crept on. Silent, slow.

The forest grew denser here. The light was dimmer, the air cooler. Tara moved with caution, her senses heightened. She could feel something in the air, a tension that hadn't been there before. And there was that smell. A dark, familiar, predatory smell.

Finally, she saw her prey. The Chasmosaurus had stopped in a small clearing, its sides heaving. It was tired, its head drooping, but it was still alert. Tara crouched low, preparing to strike. She needed to be quick, to take the dinosaur down before it could use its horns in defence.

She crouched, ready to strike.

But before she could spring forward, another presence stepped into the clearing. It was Tarok, his eyes burning with rage. He was larger than she remembered, his scales darker, his teeth bared in a snarl. He had sensed her presence and he was not pleased. This was his forest now.

Tara stepped into the clearing, rising to her full height, her eyes locked on her brother's. The Chasmosaurus, forgotten for the moment, took the opportunity to escape, lumbering away as fast as its old legs could carry it. But Tara barely noticed its departure. All her attention was on Tarok, the brother she hadn't seen since he had abandoned her to the Dromeosaurs.

Brother and sister faced each other. Neither was going to back down.

84

Chapter 13

Tara and Tarok stood motionless, sizing each other up.

Then suddenly, with a roar that echoed through the forest, Tarok lunged forward, his massive jaws snapping.

Tara dodged swiftly, her movements sharp and calculated. She had always been the quicker of the two. Tarok, larger and stronger, used brute force, his every move fueled by rage and power. They circled each other, looking for an opening.

Tarok struck first, his tail swinging with tremendous force. Tara narrowly avoided it, feeling the whoosh of air as it passed by her face. She countered with a snap of her jaws, aiming for his side, but Tarok recoiled just in time. They were evenly matched, each one's strengths balancing the other's.

The fight escalated. Tara used her speed to her advantage, darting in and out, delivering quick, precise bites. Tarok, undeterred, responded with sheer force, smashing his head into Tara's flanks.

They clashed, teeth gnashing, tails thrashing, the sound of their battle reverberating through the forest. Dust and leaves were kicked up around them, the ground beneath their feet pounded into mud.

Tarok brought his massive head down again, missing the bite, but slamming his skull into Tara's old leg injury. Tara let out a roar of pain. Her leg, though mostly healed, was still her weak point. She stumbled, her movements now hindered.

Tarok, sensing his advantage, pressed on with renewed fury, attacking her from one side, then the other, not giving her a moment to recover. Tara struggled to keep up, her leg throbbing with pain.

He was bigger, stronger, and now that he had found her weakness, he was relentless. Tara, limping and in pain, was pushed to the edge of the clearing, pinned between two old trees. She dodged another swipe of Tarok's massive jaws, but just barely.

Then, amidst the chaos, Tara saw her chance. Tarok, in his rage, had become predictable. She waited for him to strike again, to overextend himself.

And he did. With a thunderous roar, Tarok lunged at her, confident of his victory. But Tara, using the last of her strength and her cunning, sidestepped at the last moment. Tarok, unable to stop his momentum, crashed into the tree.

Stunned and dazed, Tarok tried to regain his footing, but Tara was already upon him. With a powerful push, she used her head to knock him off balance. Tarok stumbled, tried to retaliate, but it was too late.

Tara, summoning all her strength and speed, delivered a series of rapid strikes, each one more forceful than the last. She smashed and bit at her brother's back. Tarok, weakened and disoriented, couldn't fend her off.

Finally, Tarok, defeated and exhausted, had no choice but to retreat. He limped away towards the far side of the forest, and the mountains beyond.

Tara stood victorious, breathing heavily, her body aching from the fight. She had won. Turok would not return. She looked around at the forest, her forest now, and let out a triumphant roar.

Chapter 14

In the aftermath of the battle with Tarok, Tara stood tall in the heart of the forest, her breaths deep and steady. The sun was beginning to set, casting long shadows between the trees. Around her, the forest was alive with the sounds of its inhabitants.

Tara began to walk through her newly claimed territory. Her leg, though still aching, carried her forward, and her eyes took in the sights of the forest with a new perspective.

Across the river, she saw the herd of Triceratops wandering across the plains. They glanced at her warily but did not flee. A pair of Deinonychus observed her from a distance, their cunning eyes assessing this new ruler of the forest.

Reaching a familiar clearing, Tara stopped and looked around. This was where it all began, the place of her birth, where she had played with Tarok under their mother's watchful gaze.

The sky turned a brilliant hue of oranges and purples as the sun set. Tara raised her head, her senses filled with the sights and sounds of the forest at dusk. She could hear the calls of nocturnal creatures beginning their nightly routines, the rustling of leaves in the gentle breeze, and the distant roar of a river.

With a final, lingering look at the clearing, Tara turned and moved deeper into the forest. Her journey was not over; it was just another chapter in the ongoing saga of her life. But for now, she was home.

The stars began to twinkle in the night sky, watching over the forest and its queen. Tara, the Tyrannosaurus rex.

THE END.

Tara's World

68 million years ago, the world was a very different place. The land we now call North America was home to the mighty Tyrannosaurus.

The world of Tara and Tarok was filled with vast forests and wide-open plains. These places were teeming with life, from towering trees to small, scurrying creatures. The climate was warmer than today, making it a lush, green world, perfect for a young T. rex to explore.

Tyrannosaurus rex, could grow up to 40 feet long and weigh as much as an elephant. They had strong legs, massive jaws, and teeth as big as bananas.

We know about T. rex and its world through fossils. Scientists who study ancient life, dig up these fossils and put together the pieces of the past. They can tell how big T. rex was, what it ate, and even how it behaved by looking at its bones and the places they are found.

In our story, Tara and Tarok start their life in a forest. This is based on fossil finds that suggest T. rex lived in various environments, including dense forests. Their early diet of lizards and insects also comes from scientific guesses about young T. rex's diet, based on the diets of similar predators.

As Tara and Tarok grew, they started hunting larger prey. This is true for T. rex, which were apex predators, meaning they were at the top of the food chain. They probably hunted large dinosaurs like Triceratops and Edmontosaurus. We know this because of bite marks found on the fossils of these dinosaurs that match the teeth of T. rex.

The forest fire in our story is an example of the challenges dinosaurs faced. While we don't have specific evidence of forest fires during T. rex's time, scientists know natural disasters were common and would have impacted dinosaur life.

Finding their mother's body after the fire was a sad moment for Tara and Tarok. In reality, we don't have evidence of how young T. rex reacted to losing their parents. But, we do know that like many young animals, they probably relied on their parents for survival in their early years.

The encounter with an Ankylosaurus, a dinosaur covered in armour-like plates, is based on real fossils. Scientists have found T. rex fossils with injuries that could have come from fights with armoured dinosaurs. These encounters would have been dangerous and challenging for T. rex.

Tara turning to scavenging after her injury is also based on scientific studies. Some scientists believe T. rex were not just hunters but also scavengers. This means they would have eaten animals that were already dead. Evidence for this includes T. rex's strong sense of smell, which would have helped them find food.

Throughout the story, Tara and Tarok meet various other dinosaurs. These encounters are based on the types of animals that lived during the same time as T. rex. For example, the confrontation with Dromaeosaurs, small but fierce dinosaurs, adds to the story's excitement and is a glimpse into the diverse world of the Cretaceous period.

The world of the T. rex ended about 65 million years ago, in an event called the Cretaceous-Paleogene extinction when a massive asteroid crashed into the earth, eventually killing off almost all creatures larger than a fox. This event wiped out the dinosaurs, but they left behind a rich fossil record for us to discover and learn from.

Studying dinosaurs like T. rex helps us understand our world's history. It tells us how life on Earth has changed and how creatures have adapted over millions of years. It's a story that connects us all to the past.

The world of dinosaurs is still full of mysteries. Scientists continue to make new discoveries, uncovering more about these fascinating creatures. Each fossil is a piece of the puzzle, helping us understand the amazing world of the dinosaurs.

Other Animal Stories

ANIMAL STORIES: SEASON 1

TRILOBITE'S JOURNEY

A PREHISTORIC ADVENTURE BOOK

Trilobite's Journey: Chapter 1

In the cool blue waters of the Cambrian sea, Selenops the trilobite glided over the sandy floor. Her many legs moved in a wave, pushing her forward in her search for breakfast. Today, the ocean was bustling with life. Tiny creatures with shells clung to rocks, filtering food from the water around them.

Selenops' eyes, round and sharp, scanned the sea floor. She was looking for something to eat, but so was everyone else. Nearby, a group of small brachiopods were busy at work. They didn't move much, but their presence meant food was around. Other trilobites, their hard shells glinting in the filtered sunlight, scurried toward the brachiopods. They hoped to steal a bite or two.

Feeling the rumble in her belly, Selenops knew she had to find her own meal. She couldn't waste time fighting with her cousins for scraps. She moved away from the crowd, her antennae touching the ground, feeling for something else, something hidden.

Selenops' antennae twitched. They had caught a scent, a whiff of something promising. Algae! But where was it? She began to dig, her spiny legs kicking up clouds of sand. The other trilobites didn't notice. They were too busy squabbling over tiny morsels.

Finally, her efforts paid off. Beneath the sand, a patch of green algae clung to a rock, untouched and ripe for eating. Selenops' mouthparts worked quickly, tearing at the soft plant. She ate and ate, filling her stomach with the fresh algae.

With her hunger satisfied, Selenops cleaned her antennae, brushing them with her front legs. She was ready for whatever the day would bring. Her journey through the Cambrian seas was just beginning, and with a full belly, she felt like she could take on the world.

Now read on...

Printed in Great Britain
by Amazon